The Weal

Unleashing You

Christ

CW00421192

2025

Copyright © 2023 by Christopher Ford

Chapter 1: Laying the Foundation

Understanding Wealth and its Connection to Happiness

Before delving into the practical strategies to accumulate wealth, it is essential to understand the true nature of wealth and its relationship with happiness. In this book, we will explore the underlying principles that connect wealth and happiness, enabling you to create a solid foundation for your financial journey.

1.1 Defining Wealth:

Wealth encompasses more than just monetary possessions. It is a holistic concept that encompasses financial resources, personal well-being, and a sense of fulfilment. True wealth is achieved when there is an alignment between material abundance, emotional well-being, and purposeful living.

1.2 The Pursuit of Happiness:

While wealth alone does not guarantee happiness, it can contribute to certain aspects of a fulfilling life. Understanding the connection between wealth and happiness involves recognizing that financial stability provides opportunities, choices, and freedom, which can enhance overall well-being.

1.3 The Role of Mindset:

Developing a healthy mindset around wealth is crucial. Cultivate gratitude for what you have, practice mindfulness, and embrace a positive outlook on life. By adopting an abundance mindset, you open yourself up to greater possibilities and attract more opportunities for wealth creation.

1.4 Aligning Wealth with Values and Purpose:

Wealth should be pursued with a clear understanding of your personal values and life purpose. When your financial goals align with your core beliefs and passions, you are more likely to experience a sense of fulfilment and satisfaction as you progress on your wealth-building journey.

1.5 Balancing Wealth and Well-being:

Wealth should not be pursued at the expense of physical and mental well-being, relationships, or personal growth. Strive for a balanced approach that prioritizes holistic well-being while pursuing financial success. Nurture relationships, maintain self-care practices, and invest in personal development alongside wealth creation.

1.6 The Impact of Generosity:

Research consistently shows that acts of giving and generosity contribute to increased happiness. As you accumulate wealth, consider incorporating philanthropy and giving back to your community. By making a positive impact on others' lives, you enhance your own well-being and find deeper meaning in your wealth.

Understanding the connection between wealth and happiness is essential for building sustainable and fulfilling wealth. Wealth goes beyond mere financial abundance; it encompasses overall well-being, purpose, and the pursuit of a meaningful life. By aligning your financial goals with your values, maintaining a healthy mindset, and embracing a balanced approach, you can create wealth that brings you joy and contributes to your overall happiness. Remember, wealth is a tool to enhance your life and the lives of others, so use it wisely and responsibly.

Cultivating a Wealth Mindset

Developing a wealth mindset is a crucial step towards achieving financial success. It involves adopting a set of beliefs, attitudes, and habits that support wealth creation and abundance. In this section, we will explore strategies to help you cultivate a wealth mindset.

- Believe in Abundance:

Shift your perspective from scarcity to abundance. Understand that there are abundant opportunities for wealth creation and that success is not limited to a select few. Embrace the belief that there is enough wealth to go around and that you have the ability to create your own prosperity.

- Practice Gratitude:

Cultivate a sense of gratitude for what you already have. Acknowledge your current resources, achievements, and blessings. By focusing on gratitude, you attract more positive experiences and opportunities into your life.

- Embrace a Positive Attitude:

Maintain a positive attitude towards money, wealth, and financial success. Replace negative thoughts and self-limiting beliefs with empowering affirmations and thoughts of abundance. Surround yourself with positive influences, inspiring books, and motivational resources that reinforce a positive mindset.

- Set Clear Goals:

Define clear and specific financial goals. Write them down and visualize yourself achieving them. Setting goals helps you create a sense of direction and purpose, and it motivates you to take action towards your desired financial outcomes.

- Take Calculated Risks:

Embrace calculated risks as a means to grow your wealth. Understand that some level of risk is necessary for progress and wealth accumulation. Educate yourself about potential risks, weigh the pros and cons, and take informed risks that align with your goals and risk tolerance.

- Seek Continuous Learning:

Commit to lifelong learning and personal growth. Stay updated on industry trends, financial markets, and new opportunities. Read books, attend seminars, listen to podcasts, and surround yourself with knowledgeable individuals who can expand your understanding of wealth creation.

- Practice Persistence and Resilience:

Building wealth is a journey that involves ups and downs. Develop resilience and persistence to overcome challenges and setbacks. Learn from failures, adjust your strategies, and keep moving forward with determination.

- Surround Yourself with Like-Minded Individuals:

Surround yourself with individuals who have a positive mindset towards wealth and success. Engage in networking events, join mastermind groups, or seek out mentors who can provide guidance and support on your wealth-building journey.

- Take Ownership of Your Finances:

Take responsibility for your financial decisions and actions. Educate yourself about personal finance, budgeting, investing, and wealth management. Avoid excessive reliance on others for financial advice and take an active role in managing your money.

- Give Back:

Embrace the power of giving back. Practice philanthropy and contribute to causes you care about. Recognize that generosity and helping others can enhance your own sense of abundance and create a positive impact on the world.

Remember, cultivating a wealth mindset is an ongoing practice. Be patient with yourself, celebrate small victories, and consistently reinforce positive beliefs and habits. By adopting a wealth mindset, you will attract opportunities, take purposeful actions, and pave the way for financial abundance and success.

Goal Setting

Setting clear financial goals is a crucial step towards achieving financial success. Goals provide direction, motivation, and a framework for making sound financial decisions. In this section, we will explore effective strategies for setting financial goals and actionable steps to achieve them.

- Reflect on Your Values and Priorities:

Start by reflecting on your values, priorities, and what you want to achieve in life. Consider both short-term and long-term aspirations. Your financial goals should align with your personal values and contribute to your overall vision of a fulfilling life.

- Make Goals Specific and Measurable:

Ensure that your financial goals are specific and measurable. For example, instead of setting a vague goal like "Save more money," define a specific target such as "Save $10,000 for an emergency fund within the next year." Clear and measurable goals enable you to track progress and stay motivated.

- Break Goals Down into Smaller Milestones:

Break down larger goals into smaller, achievable milestones. This approach makes your goals more manageable and provides a sense of progress along the way. Each milestone reached reinforces your commitment and motivates you to keep moving forward.

- Set Realistic and Time-Bound Goals:

Ensure that your financial goals are realistic and attainable within a given timeframe. Consider your current financial situation, income, expenses, and any other relevant factors. Be ambitious but also practical. Set deadlines for achieving your goals, as they create a sense of urgency and help you stay focused.

- Write Down Your Goals:

Put your financial goals in writing. The act of writing makes them more tangible and increases your commitment. Keep your written goals somewhere visible, such as a vision board or a dedicated journal. Regularly review and revisit them to stay on track.

- Create an Action Plan:

Develop a detailed action plan outlining the specific steps needed to achieve each financial goal. Break down the plan into actionable tasks, assign deadlines, and prioritize them accordingly. Having a clear plan allows you to track progress, make adjustments when necessary, and stay organized.

- Track Your Finances:

Maintain a budget and track your expenses. Regularly review your income and spending to ensure you're staying on track towards your goals. Use financial tools and apps to simplify tracking and gain a clear understanding of your financial situation.

- Seek Expert Advice:

Consider consulting with a financial advisor or planner to get professional guidance on setting and achieving your financial goals. They can provide valuable insights, offer personalized strategies, and help you navigate complex financial decisions.

- Stay Disciplined and Stay the Course:

Achieving financial goals requires discipline and perseverance. Stay committed to your goals, even when faced with challenges or setbacks. Keep your long-term vision in mind and remind yourself of the reasons behind your goals. Be prepared to make necessary sacrifices and stay focused on the bigger picture.

- Celebrate Milestones and Adjust as Needed:

Celebrate each milestone you achieve along the way. Recognize and reward yourself for your progress, as it reinforces your motivation and commitment. Be open to adjusting your goals if circumstances change or new opportunities arise. Regularly review and reassess your goals to ensure they remain relevant and aligned with your evolving priorities.

Remember, setting and achieving financial goals is an ongoing process. Regularly review and update your goals as you progress. Stay adaptable, remain focused, and embrace the journey towards financial success. With dedication and persistence, you can turn your financial aspirations into reality.

Chapter 2: Building Multiple Streams of Income

Leveraging Your Skills and Talents

Your unique skills and talents can be valuable assets in generating income and creating opportunities for financial success. By leveraging what you excel at, you can pursue fulfilling ventures and increase your earning potential. Here are some steps to help you harness your skills and talents to make money:

- Identify Your Skills and Talents:

Take time to assess and identify your skills, talents, and areas of expertise. Consider both hard skills (specific technical abilities) and soft skills (interpersonal and transferable skills). Reflect on activities you enjoy and excel at, as they can form the foundation for monetizing your talents.

- Research Market Demand:

Research the market demand for the skills and talents you possess. Identify industries, niches, or target audiences that value and are willing to pay for what you offer. Explore online job boards, freelance platforms, and networking events to gain insights into current opportunities.

- Evaluate Monetization Options:

Determine how you can monetize your skills and talents effectively. Consider various avenues such as freelancing, consulting, teaching, creating digital products, or starting your own business. Assess the pros and cons of each option based on your skills, resources, and desired level of involvement.

- Develop a Value Proposition:

Craft a clear value proposition that highlights the unique value you bring to potential clients or customers. Clearly articulate how your skills and talents can solve their problems, enhance their businesses, or fulfil their needs. Focus on communicating the benefits and outcomes you can deliver.

- Build Your Brand and Online Presence:

Create a professional brand that showcases your skills and talents. Develop a compelling resume or portfolio, build a professional website, and establish a strong online presence through social media platforms, relevant forums, and industry-specific communities. Consistently demonstrate your expertise and engage with your target audience.

- Network and Collaborate:

Network with individuals and businesses in your field or industry. Attend industry events, join professional associations, and actively seek opportunities to collaborate with others. Building relationships and connections can lead to referrals, partnerships, and new income-generating ventures.

- Continuous Skill Development:

Invest in continuous learning and skill development to enhance your existing talents. Stay updated on industry trends, new technologies, and emerging best practices. Take courses, attend workshops, and participate in relevant training programs to expand your skill set and remain competitive.

- Market Yourself Effectively:

Master the art of self-promotion and marketing. Develop a strong elevator pitch that effectively communicates your skills, talents, and unique selling points. Utilize online marketing strategies such as content creation, social media marketing, and search engine optimization to reach a broader audience.

- Provide Excellent Service or Products:

Deliver exceptional service or high-quality products that exceed customer expectations. Prioritize customer satisfaction, address feedback, and continuously improve your offerings. Building a reputation for excellence will lead to repeat business, referrals, and positive word-of-mouth recommendations.

- Adapt and Diversify:

Stay adaptable and open to new opportunities. Explore different ways to monetize your skills and talents, and be willing to adapt to market changes. Consider diversifying your income streams by offering a range of services, targeting different client segments, or exploring new markets.

Remember, turning your skills and talents into a profitable venture requires dedication, perseverance, and continuous improvement. Embrace your uniqueness, market yourself effectively, and provide value to others. With time and effort, you can leverage your skills and talents to create a fulfilling and financially rewarding career.

Exploring Entrepreneurship

Starting and managing a successful business requires careful planning, strategic decision-making, and effective execution. While the journey can be challenging, it can also be highly rewarding. Here are key steps to help you start and manage a successful business:

- Develop a Business Idea:

Identify a business idea that aligns with your passions, skills, and market demand. Conduct thorough market research to validate your idea, assess competition, and understand your target audience's needs and preferences.

- Create a Business Plan:

Develop a comprehensive business plan that outlines your mission, vision, target market, products or services, marketing strategies, financial projections, and operational details. A well-crafted business plan serves as a roadmap for your business and helps secure funding if needed.

- Secure Adequate Financing:

Determine the financial resources required to start and sustain your business. Explore different funding options such as personal savings, loans, grants, or investors. Create a detailed financial plan that includes startup costs, working capital, and anticipated cash flow.

- Register Your Business:

Choose a suitable legal structure for your business (e.g., sole proprietorship, partnership, corporation) and register it with the appropriate government authorities. Obtain any necessary licenses, permits, or certifications to operate legally and comply with regulatory requirements.

- Set Up Your Operations:

Establish your physical or virtual business location, acquire necessary equipment and technology, and set up efficient operational processes. Secure reliable suppliers or vendors and establish relationships with them. Consider building a team or hiring employees as your business grows.

- Develop a Marketing Strategy:

Craft a comprehensive marketing strategy to promote your products or services. Define your unique selling proposition, identify target customers, and create a strong brand identity. Utilize online and offline marketing channels to reach and engage your target audience effectively.

- Build a Strong Online Presence:

In today's digital age, establishing an online presence is crucial. Build a professional website, optimize it for search engines, and leverage social media platforms to connect with your target audience. Develop compelling content and engage with potential customers through relevant online channels.

- Establish Effective Financial Management:

Implement sound financial management practices from the start. Keep accurate records of income and expenses, set up a bookkeeping system, and regularly review financial statements. Monitor cash flow, manage budgets, and seek professional advice if necessary.

- Provide Excellent Customer Service:

Deliver exceptional customer service to build customer loyalty and gain a competitive edge. Focus on understanding and meeting customer needs, responding to feedback promptly, and continuously improving your products or services based on customer insights.

- Continuously Innovate and Adapt:

Stay agile and be open to change. Continuously evaluate market trends, customer preferences, and competitive landscape. Innovate your products, services, and business processes to stay relevant and meet evolving customer demands.

- Seek Professional Advice and Mentorship:

Don't hesitate to seek guidance from experienced entrepreneurs, mentors, or business consultants. Their expertise and insights can provide valuable guidance and help you navigate challenges effectively.

- Monitor Key Performance Indicators:

Identify key performance indicators (KPIs) that align with your business goals and regularly track them. Monitor financial metrics, sales figures, customer satisfaction, and other relevant data. Use these insights to make informed decisions and adjust your strategies as needed.

Remember, building a successful business requires time, effort, and perseverance. Stay focused, stay adaptable, and continuously learn from both successes and failures. By following these steps and staying committed to your vision, you can increase your chances of starting and managing a thriving business.

Investing for Passive Income

Generating passive income involves setting up income streams that require minimal ongoing effort or time once established. While it may require upfront work and investment, passive income can provide financial stability and freedom. Here are several ways to generate passive income:

- Rental Properties:

Invest in real estate properties, such as residential or commercial buildings, and earn rental income. Property management companies can handle tenant interactions and property maintenance on your behalf, making it a relatively passive income source.

- Dividend Stocks and Mutual Funds:

Invest in dividend-paying stocks or mutual funds. Dividends are periodic payouts distributed to shareholders, providing passive income. Research and choose reputable companies or funds that consistently deliver dividends and align with your investment goals.

- Peer-to-Peer Lending:

Participate in peer-to-peer lending platforms where you lend money to individuals or businesses in return for interest payments. These platforms handle the loan origination, repayment, and associated tasks, making it a passive investment option.

- Digital Products and Royalties:

Create and sell digital products, such as e-books, online courses, stock photography, or music. Once the initial creation is complete, these products can generate passive income as they can be sold repeatedly without requiring direct involvement.

- Affiliate Marketing:

Promote other people's products or services through affiliate marketing programs. Earn commissions when someone makes a purchase through your unique referral link. Develop an online platform, such as a blog or website, to attract visitors and drive conversions.

- Create and License Intellectual Property:

Develop and license intellectual property, such as patents, trademarks, or copyrights. You can earn royalties from licensing agreements when others use your intellectual property, generating passive income over time.

- Automated Online Businesses:

Establish an automated online business, such as drop shipping, e-commerce stores, or software-as-a-service (SaaS) platforms. These businesses can be set up to operate with minimal manual intervention once the initial setup and marketing are completed.

- Real Estate Investment Trusts (REITs):

Invest in REITs, which are companies that own and manage income-generating real estate properties. By purchasing shares in a REIT, you can earn passive income from rental income and property appreciation without directly owning the properties.

- High-Yield Savings Accounts or Certificates of Deposit (CDs):

Park your savings in high-yield savings accounts or CDs offered by banks. These accounts provide regular interest payments on your deposited funds, creating passive income with minimal risk.

- Rent Out Assets:

Rent out assets you own, such as a car, parking space, storage unit, or equipment. Online platforms and marketplaces make it easier to connect with potential renters, allowing you to generate passive income from underutilized assets.

Remember, generating passive income often requires upfront investment, research, and monitoring. Choose the methods that align with your financial goals, risk tolerance, and available resources. Diversify your passive income streams to mitigate risk and create a more stable financial foundation.

The Power of Passive Income

Passive income streams play a significant role in building long-term wealth. Here's how they contribute to your financial journey:

1. Income Diversification: Passive income streams provide an additional source of income beyond traditional employment or active business ventures. By diversifying your income sources, you reduce reliance on a single source and create a more stable financial foundation.
2. Financial Stability: Passive income streams provide a consistent flow of income, even when you're not actively working. This stability helps cover living expenses, meet financial goals, and create a buffer for unexpected expenses or economic downturns.
3. Time and Location Freedom: Passive income streams require minimal ongoing effort once established. This allows you to

have more freedom over your time and location. You can spend your time pursuing other interests, engaging in meaningful activities, or even exploring new business ventures.

4. Accelerated Wealth Growth: Passive income can accelerate the growth of your wealth by compounding over time. As your passive income streams increase, you can reinvest the earnings, generating even more income and building wealth at an accelerated rate.

5. Asset Appreciation: Certain passive income sources, such as real estate or stocks, can appreciate in value over time. This not only generates income but also leads to capital appreciation, increasing your overall net worth and contributing to long-term wealth accumulation.

6. Financial Independence and Retirement Planning: Passive income streams are key to achieving financial independence and early retirement. By building a portfolio of passive income sources, you can generate enough income to cover your expenses without relying on traditional employment. This enables you to have more control over your lifestyle and retirement goals.

7. Legacy and Wealth Transfer: Passive income streams can create a legacy and facilitate wealth transfer to future generations. By building and managing income-generating assets, you can create a sustainable source of wealth that can be passed down to your heirs, providing financial security for your family.

8. Reinvestment and Business Expansion: As passive income grows, you have the option to reinvest the earnings into expanding existing income streams or exploring new ventures. This reinvestment can lead to further growth and diversification of your passive income portfolio, contributing to long-term wealth building.

It's important to note that building passive income streams requires initial effort, investment, and continuous monitoring. Each income stream may have its own risks and considerations. Proper due diligence, research, and ongoing management are crucial for maximizing the potential of passive income and ensuring its contribution to long-term wealth.

Chapter 3: Mastering Financial Literacy

Personal Finance Management

Effectively managing your finances through budgeting, saving, and debt management is crucial for achieving financial stability and building wealth. Here are key steps to help you in these areas:

- Create a Budget:

  Develop a budget by tracking your income and expenses. Identify fixed expenses (e.g., rent, utilities) and variable expenses (e.g., groceries, entertainment). Set realistic spending limits in each category and prioritize essential expenses. Use budgeting apps or spreadsheets to streamline the process.

- Track and Review Expenses:

  Regularly track and review your expenses to ensure they align with your budget. Identify areas where you can cut back on non-essential spending and make adjustments as needed. Consider using expense tracking apps or setting up alerts for overspending.

- Save for Emergencies:

  Build an emergency fund to cover unexpected expenses or financial setbacks. Aim to save three to six months' worth of living expenses. Set up automatic transfers to a dedicated savings account and treat saving as a regular expense. Prioritize your emergency fund to provide a safety net.

- Set Savings Goals:

Establish short-term and long-term savings goals. Determine specific amounts and timelines for each goal. Whether it's saving for a down payment on a house, a vacation, or retirement, having clear goals provides motivation and helps you stay on track.

- Prioritize Debt Repayment:

Create a debt repayment plan. List all your debts, including credit cards, loans, and student debt. Prioritize them based on interest rates and pay off high-interest debts first while making minimum payments on other debts. Consider debt consolidation or balance transfer options to simplify repayment and reduce interest costs.

- Minimize New Debt:

Avoid accumulating new debt whenever possible. Limit credit card usage and pay off balances in full each month to avoid interest charges. Before taking on new debt, carefully evaluate the necessity and potential impact on your overall financial situation.

- Negotiate Lower Interest Rates:

Contact creditors and negotiate lower interest rates or explore debt refinancing options. Lower interest rates can significantly reduce the total cost of debt repayment and help you become debt-free sooner.

- Seek Professional Guidance:

If you're overwhelmed with debt or struggling to manage your finances, consider seeking help from a financial advisor or credit counselling service. They can provide personalized guidance, help you create a debt management plan, and offer strategies for improving your financial situation.

- Automate Savings and Bill Payments:

Set up automatic transfers to savings accounts to ensure consistent saving. Automate bill payments to avoid late fees or missed payments. This helps streamline your finances and ensures that saving and debt repayment are prioritized.

- Review and Adjust Regularly:

Regularly review your budget, savings progress, and debt repayment strategy. Make adjustments as necessary to stay on track and accommodate any changes in your financial situation or goals. Regularly monitoring and adjusting your finances is essential for long-term success.

Remember, managing your finances requires discipline, commitment, and ongoing attention. Be patient with your progress and stay focused on your long-term financial goals. By implementing these strategies, you can effectively finance your budget, save for the future, and manage debt to achieve financial stability and build wealth over time.

Understanding Taxes

Financial tax strategies are essential for optimizing your tax situation, maximizing deductions, and minimizing your overall tax liability. Here are several key tax strategies to consider:

- Understand Tax Laws and Regulations:

Stay informed about tax laws and regulations relevant to your country or region. Regularly review updates and changes to tax codes to ensure compliance and take advantage of available deductions or credits.

- Take Advantage of Tax-Advantaged Accounts:

Contribute to tax-advantaged accounts such as Individual Retirement Accounts (IRAs), 401(k)s, or similar retirement plans. These accounts offer tax benefits such as tax-deferred growth or tax-free withdrawals, reducing your current or future tax liability.

- Utilize Tax Deductions:

Identify and utilize tax deductions available to you. Some common deductions include mortgage interest, property taxes, student loan interest, medical expenses, charitable contributions, and business expenses (for self-employed individuals). Keep detailed records and gather necessary documentation to support your deductions.

- Maximize Retirement Contributions:

Contribute the maximum allowable amount to your retirement accounts. Not only does this help secure your financial future, but it can also provide immediate tax benefits by reducing your taxable income.

- Consider Tax Loss Harvesting:

If you have investments, consider tax loss harvesting. This strategy involves selling investments that have declined in value to offset capital gains and potentially reduce your tax liability. Be aware of tax rules regarding capital gains and losses, including the wash-sale rule.

- Optimize Timing of Income and Deductions:

Manage the timing of your income and deductions to optimize your tax situation. For example, if you expect to be in a lower tax bracket in the coming year, consider deferring income to reduce your current tax liability. Conversely, if you anticipate being in a higher tax bracket, accelerate deductions into the current year.

- Keep Business and Personal Finances Separate:

If you run a business, keep your business and personal finances separate. Establish a separate business bank account, track business expenses diligently, and maintain accurate records. This separation helps you claim all eligible business deductions and avoids potential issues during tax filings.

- Consult with a Tax Professional:

Consider seeking guidance from a tax professional, such as a certified public accountant (CPA) or tax advisor. They can provide personalized advice, help you navigate complex tax matters, and ensure compliance with applicable tax laws. A professional can also identify specific strategies and deductions that align with your financial situation.

- Stay Organized and Maintain Documentation:

Maintain organized records and documentation of your financial transactions, expenses, and tax-related information. This includes receipts, invoices, bank statements, and investment records. Organized documentation simplifies tax preparation, helps support your deductions, and ensures accuracy during tax filings.

- Regularly Review and Adjust:

Regularly review your financial situation, tax strategies, and goals. As your circumstances change, adjust your tax strategies accordingly. Regularly reviewing and optimizing your tax planning ensures you take advantage of available opportunities and minimize your tax liability.

Remember, tax laws and regulations can be complex and vary by jurisdiction. It's important to consult with a qualified tax professional to tailor tax strategies to your specific situation and ensure compliance with applicable laws.

Smart Banking

Optimizing your savings and effectively managing loans are essential for achieving financial stability and maximizing your financial resources. Here are some strategies to help you optimize your savings and manage loans effectively:

- Prioritize Saving:

Make saving a priority by setting a specific savings goal and allocating a portion of your income towards it. Treat savings as a non-negotiable expense and automate regular contributions to your savings account. Consistency is key in building a healthy savings habit.

- Establish an Emergency Fund:

Create an emergency fund to cover unexpected expenses or financial setbacks. Aim to save three to six months' worth of living expenses. This fund provides a financial safety net, reducing the need to rely on loans or credit cards during emergencies.

- Pay Yourself First:

Allocate a percentage of your income towards savings before allocating funds for other expenses. By paying yourself first, you prioritize saving and build a strong financial foundation.

- Reduce Unnecessary Expenses:

Identify and cut back on unnecessary expenses in your budget. Review your spending habits and identify areas where you can reduce costs. Consider negotiating bills, switching to more affordable alternatives, or eliminating non-essential expenditures to free up funds for savings or debt repayment.

- Automate Savings:

Set up automatic transfers from your checking account to your savings account. By automating your savings, you remove the temptation to spend the money and ensure consistent contributions towards your financial goals.

- Consolidate and Refinance Loans:

If you have multiple loans, consider consolidating them into one loan with a lower interest rate. This can simplify your repayment process and potentially reduce your overall interest costs. Additionally, refinancing high-interest loans, such as student loans or mortgages, can help lower your monthly payments and save money over time.

- Accelerate Loan Repayment:

To manage loans effectively, consider accelerating repayment. Pay more than the minimum required payment each month to reduce the principal balance faster and minimize interest charges. Prioritize higher-interest loans first while making minimum payments on others.

- Negotiate Loan Terms:

When obtaining a loan, negotiate terms that work in your favour. Compare offers from different lenders, negotiate interest rates, and review loan terms and conditions. Small adjustments in interest rates or loan terms can have a significant impact on the total cost of borrowing.

- Explore Loan Forgiveness Programs:

If you have student loans, investigate loan forgiveness or repayment assistance programs that you may qualify for based on your profession, location, or income. These programs can help reduce your loan burden over time.

- Seek Professional Advice:

If you are struggling to manage your loans or optimize your savings, consider seeking guidance from a financial advisor or credit counselling service. They can provide personalized advice, help you create a repayment plan, and offer strategies for maximizing your savings potential.

- Regularly Review and Adjust:

Regularly review your savings progress and loan repayment strategy. Assess your financial situation, goals, and any changes that may impact your approach. Adjust your strategies as needed to stay on track and make the most of your financial resources.

Remember, optimizing savings and managing loans require discipline, commitment, and ongoing attention. Consistently review your financial situation, track your progress, and make adjustments as necessary to achieve your financial goals and build a strong financial future.

Insurance and Risk Management

Protecting your wealth from potential risks and uncertainties is an essential aspect of financial planning. Insurance and risk mitigation strategies can provide a safety net, preserve your assets, and ensure long-term financial security. Here are some key considerations for safeguarding wealth:

- Evaluate Insurance Needs:

Assess your insurance needs and determine the types of coverage required to protect your assets and mitigate risks. Common types of insurance include:

Health Insurance: Obtain comprehensive health insurance coverage to protect against high medical expenses and ensure access to quality healthcare.

Life Insurance: Consider life insurance to provide financial protection for your loved ones in the event of your passing. Choose a policy that aligns with your specific needs and financial goals.

Property and Casualty Insurance: Protect your property and belongings through homeowners, renters, or property insurance. Consider additional coverage for natural disasters, theft, or liability.

Auto Insurance: Comply with legal requirements and protect against potential accidents, damage, or theft by having adequate auto insurance coverage.

Disability Insurance: Secure disability insurance to provide income replacement in case of a disabling injury or illness that prevents you from working.

- Work with an Insurance Professional:

Consult an insurance professional or broker to assess your specific insurance needs and identify appropriate coverage options. They can provide insights into available policies, help you understand the terms and conditions, and guide you in selecting the right coverage for your circumstances.

- Maintain Adequate Coverage:

Regularly review your insurance policies to ensure you have adequate coverage for your changing circumstances. Update policies as necessary to reflect changes in assets, lifestyle, or family situation. Don't overlook policy renewals and make sure coverage remains in force.

- Mitigate Liability Risks:

Protect your wealth by mitigating potential liability risks. Consider liability insurance, such as umbrella insurance, to provide additional protection beyond the limits of your primary policies. Also, practice responsible behaviour and take precautions to minimize the risk of accidents or lawsuits.

- Asset Protection Strategies:

Explore legal strategies to protect your assets, such as trusts, limited liability companies (LLCs), or other legal structures. These entities can offer an additional layer of protection against potential creditors, lawsuits, or other financial liabilities. Consult with an attorney specializing in asset protection for guidance.

- Diversify Investments:

Diversify your investment portfolio to reduce exposure to specific risks. Spread your investments across various asset classes, industries, and geographical locations. Diversification helps mitigate the impact of market volatility and potential losses.

- Estate Planning:

Develop a comprehensive estate plan to protect and distribute your wealth according to your wishes. Create a will, establish trusts, designate beneficiaries, and plan for potential estate taxes. Work with an estate planning attorney to ensure your assets are protected and transition smoothly to the next generation.

- Maintain an Emergency Fund:

Build and maintain an emergency fund to protect against unexpected financial setbacks. This fund should cover three to six months' worth of living expenses and serve as a buffer during job loss, medical emergencies, or other unforeseen circumstances.

- Risk Assessment and Mitigation:

Regularly assess potential risks that could impact your wealth. Identify vulnerabilities and develop strategies to mitigate those risks. This might include cybersecurity measures, disaster preparedness plans, or appropriate insurance coverage.

- Stay Informed:

Stay updated on evolving risks, insurance options, and best practices for wealth protection. Continuously educate yourself on new insurance products, changes in regulations, and risk management techniques. Seek advice from trusted professionals and stay proactive in safeguarding your wealth.

Remember, every individual's risk profile and insurance needs are unique. Work with professionals in the insurance and legal fields to tailor insurance coverage and risk mitigation strategies to your specific circumstances. By safeguarding your wealth through insurance and risk mitigation, you can protect your assets, ensure financial stability, and preserve your long-term financial well-being.

Chapter 4: Embracing the Digital Age

Online Business Opportunities

E-commerce, digital marketing, and freelancing are all interconnected and offer tremendous opportunities for individuals to establish successful online businesses, promote products or services, and work independently. Here's an overview of each area:

- E-commerce:

E-commerce refers to the buying and selling of goods or services online. It involves setting up an online store or platform to showcase products, process transactions, and facilitate customer interactions. Key aspects of e-commerce include:

a. Choosing a Niche: Select a specific product or service niche that aligns with market demand and your interests. Conduct market research to identify target customers and competitors.

b. Building an Online Store: Establish an online presence through an e-commerce platform or website. Customize the design, optimize the user experience, and integrate secure payment options.

c. Product Sourcing or Creation: Determine how you will source products, whether through manufacturing, drop shipping, or working with suppliers. Alternatively, create your own products or offer digital goods or services.

d. Marketing and Promotion: Develop marketing strategies to attract customers and drive traffic to your online store. Utilize digital marketing techniques such as search engine optimization (SEO), social media marketing, email marketing, and paid advertising to increase visibility and generate sales.

e. Order Fulfilment and Customer Service: Ensure efficient order fulfilment, shipping, and handling of customer inquiries. Provide excellent customer service to build loyalty and encourage positive reviews.

- Digital Marketing:

Digital marketing encompasses various strategies and tactics used to promote products, services, or brands online. It involves leveraging digital channels and technologies to reach and engage target audiences. Key components of digital marketing include:

a. Search Engine Optimization (SEO): Optimize your website or online content to rank higher in search engine results, increasing organic visibility and driving targeted traffic.

b. Content Marketing: Create valuable and relevant content, such as blog posts, videos, or infographics, to attract and engage your target audience. Share content on your website, social media platforms, and other online channels.

c. Social Media Marketing: Leverage social media platforms to build brand awareness, engage with your audience, and promote your products or services. Develop a social media strategy, create compelling content, and utilize paid advertising options to reach a wider audience.

d. Email Marketing: Build an email list and use targeted email campaigns to nurture leads, promote products, and drive conversions. Personalize content, segment your audience, and measure campaign performance.

e. Pay-per-Click (PPC) Advertising: Run paid advertising campaigns on platforms like Google Ads or social media networks to drive targeted traffic to your website or online store. Set a budget, optimize ad campaigns, and track performance metrics.

f. Analytics and Data Analysis: Utilize analytics tools to measure the effectiveness of your digital marketing efforts. Analyse data to make informed decisions, optimize strategies, and improve campaign performance.

- Freelancing:

Freelancing involves offering your skills and services as an independent contractor to clients or businesses on a project basis. It provides flexibility and the opportunity to work on a variety of projects in different industries. Key aspects of freelancing include:

a. Identify Your Skills: Determine the specific skills or services you can offer as a freelancer. This could include writing, graphic design, web development, marketing, consulting, or other specialized expertise.

b. Build Your Portfolio: Showcase your previous work and projects in a portfolio to demonstrate your capabilities to potential clients. Create a professional website or online platform to showcase your skills and expertise.

c. Identify Target Clients and Niche: Define your target clients and focus on a specific niche to differentiate yourself and attract clients with specific needs.

d. Marketing and Networking: Promote your freelance services through various channels, such as social media, professional networks, freelance platforms, and your own website. Attend industry events, engage in networking, and leverage word-of-mouth referrals.

e. Pricing and Contracts: Determine your pricing structure and create clear contracts or agreements outlining project scope, deliverables, timelines, and payment terms. Ensure that you establish a fair pricing model that aligns with your skills and the value you provide.

f. Client Relationship Management: Provide exceptional client service, communicate effectively, and deliver projects on time and within budget. Build long-term relationships with clients to encourage repeat business and referrals.

Remember, e-commerce, digital marketing, and freelancing are dynamic fields that require continuous learning, adaptation, and staying up to date with industry trends. Embrace ongoing professional development, refine your skills, and leverage digital tools and resources to thrive in these areas.

Investing in Cryptocurrencies

Investing in cryptocurrency can offer opportunities for potential growth and diversification in your investment portfolio. However, it's important to approach cryptocurrency investing with caution and make informed decisions. Here are key considerations when investing in cryptocurrency:

- Educate Yourself:

Before investing, take the time to understand the fundamentals of cryptocurrencies, blockchain technology, and the specific cryptocurrency you are interested in. Research reputable sources, read whitepapers, and stay informed about market trends and regulatory developments.

- Diversify Your Portfolio:

Cryptocurrency should be seen as a part of a diversified investment portfolio, rather than the sole focus of your investments. Spread your investments across different asset classes, such as stocks, bonds, real estate, and traditional currencies, to manage risk effectively.

- Start with a Small Investment:

Consider starting with a small portion of your investment capital allocated to cryptocurrency. This approach allows you to gain experience, assess your risk tolerance, and understand the market dynamics without putting a significant portion of your wealth at risk.

- Choose Established Cryptocurrencies:

Focus on established cryptocurrencies with a solid track record, large market capitalization, and widespread adoption. Bitcoin (BTC) and Ethereum (ETH) are examples of well-known and widely used cryptocurrencies.

- Research the Project and Team:

Conduct thorough research on the specific cryptocurrency project and its development team. Evaluate the technology, use case, partnerships, and community support. Look for transparency, a strong roadmap, and an active development team.

- Understand the Risks:

Cryptocurrency investments come with inherent risks, including volatility, regulatory uncertainty, cybersecurity threats, and market manipulation. Be prepared for significant price fluctuations and potential loss of capital. Only invest what you can afford to lose.

- Choose a Reliable Exchange:

Select a reputable cryptocurrency exchange to buy, sell, and store your cryptocurrencies. Look for exchanges with strong security measures, a user-friendly interface, and a solid reputation. Conduct due diligence and consider factors like liquidity, fees, and customer support.

- Secure Your Investments:

Implement robust security measures to protect your cryptocurrency investments. Use hardware wallets or secure digital wallets to store your coins offline. Enable two-factor authentication (2FA) for added security. Be cautious of phishing attempts and scams.

- Stay Informed and Monitor:

Stay updated on market news, regulatory developments, and technological advancements in the cryptocurrency space. Regularly monitor your investments, but avoid making impulsive decisions based on short-term market fluctuations.

- Consider Professional Advice:

If you are unsure about investing in cryptocurrency or need expert guidance, consult with a financial advisor who has experience in the cryptocurrency market. They can provide personalized advice and help you navigate the complexities of cryptocurrency investing.

Remember, cryptocurrency markets are highly volatile, and investing in cryptocurrencies carries inherent risks. It's crucial to approach cryptocurrency investing with a long-term perspective, do thorough research, and make informed decisions based on your risk tolerance and investment goals.

The Sharing Economy

Peer-to-peer income generation refers to earning income through direct interactions with individuals or peers, rather than relying on traditional employment or business models. It involves leveraging your skills, resources, or assets to provide products, services, or value to others in exchange for payment. Here are some peer-to-peer income generation ideas:

- Freelancing or Consulting:

Offer your skills and expertise on a freelance or consulting basis. This could include writing, graphic design, programming, marketing, coaching, or any other specialized service. Platforms like Upwork, Fiverr, or LinkedIn can help connect you with potential clients.

- Renting or Sharing Assets:

Rent out your physical assets or resources to earn income. This could include renting out a spare room on platforms like Airbnb, sharing your car through services like Turo or Getaround, or even renting out equipment or tools to individuals or businesses.

- Peer-to-Peer Lending:

Participate in peer-to-peer lending platforms where you lend money to individuals or businesses in return for interest payments. Online platforms facilitate the borrowing and lending process, connecting lenders directly with borrowers.

- Sharing Economy Platforms:

Join sharing economy platforms where you can offer services, such as pet sitting, dog walking, house cleaning, gardening, or errand running. Platforms like TaskRabbit, Rover, or Thumbtack connect service providers with individuals in need of assistance.

- Teaching or Tutoring:

Leverage your knowledge and skills to offer teaching or tutoring services. This could be done in person or online, through platforms like VIPKid or Teachable. You can teach subjects like languages, music, academic subjects, or specialized skills.

- Arts and Crafts:

Create and sell handmade products or crafts through online marketplaces like Etsy. If you have artistic talents, such as painting, woodworking, or jewellery making, you can generate income by selling your creations directly to customers.

- Consulting or Coaching:

If you have expertise in a specific field, offer consulting or coaching services to individuals or businesses. This could be in areas like business strategy, personal finance, career development, or fitness and wellness. Develop a niche and market your services accordingly.

- Online Content Creation:

Monetize your knowledge or creativity by creating online content. Start a blog, YouTube channel, or podcast where you share valuable information, insights, or entertainment. Earn income through advertising, sponsorships, affiliate marketing, or offering premium content.

- Renting Space or Equipment:

If you have unused space, such as a garage, storage room, or office space, consider renting it out to individuals or businesses. Additionally, if you own specialized equipment that others might need on a temporary basis, you can rent it out to them.

- Personalized Services:

Offer personalized services tailored to individuals' needs and preferences. This could include personal shopping, event planning, meal preparation, organizing, or life coaching. Identify specific pain points or challenges that people face and provide solutions.

Remember to consider legal and regulatory requirements, protect your assets, and maintain professionalism and high-quality service in your peer-to-peer income generation activities. Establish clear terms of service or agreements, communicate effectively with your clients or customers, and continuously seek opportunities to improve and expand your offerings.

Harnessing the Power of social media

Social media personal brands present a wealth of income opportunities for individuals who can effectively leverage their online presence, expertise, and influence. Here's a closer look at how personal brands on social media can lead to income generation:

- Sponsored Content and Brand Partnerships:

As a social media influencer or personal brand, you can collaborate with brands and businesses to promote their products or services. This can involve sponsored posts, product reviews, endorsements, or brand ambassadorships. Brands may compensate you with monetary payments, free products, or affiliate commissions.

- Ad Revenue:

If you have a significant following on platforms like YouTube or TikTok, you can monetize your content through ad revenue. Platforms may place ads before or during your videos, and you receive a portion of the revenue generated based on views or ad clicks.

- Affiliate Marketing:

Promote products or services through affiliate marketing. You can share customized referral links or discount codes with your audience. When someone makes a purchase using your link or code, you earn a commission. Affiliate marketing works well for personal brands in niches like fashion, beauty, fitness, or technology.

- Digital Products and Services:

Create and sell digital products or services related to your expertise. Examples include e-books, online courses, templates, coaching sessions, or consulting services. Your personal brand and authority in your niche can help attract customers and generate income from these offerings.

- Sponsored Events and Speaking Engagements:

As your personal brand grows, you may be invited to speak at events, conferences, or workshops. These speaking engagements can provide income opportunities, as organizers often pay speakers for sharing their knowledge and insights with the audience.

- Crowdfunding and Donations:

If your personal brand aligns with a cause or purpose, you can explore crowdfunding platforms or accept donations from your followers. This method works well for content creators, artists, or individuals passionate about social impact.

- Product or Merchandise Sales:

Develop and sell your own branded merchandise, such as clothing, accessories, or merchandise related to your personal brand. E-commerce platforms, social media, or your own website can facilitate the sales and distribution process.

- Collaborative Projects and Joint Ventures:

Collaborate with other influencers, content creators, or entrepreneurs on joint projects. This could involve co-creating content, hosting events or workshops together, or launching joint ventures. Combining your influence and expertise can unlock new income opportunities and expand your reach.

- Personalized Coaching or Consulting:

Leverage your personal brand to offer personalized coaching, consulting, or mentoring services. This can be in areas like business, fitness, personal development, or any field where you have expertise. Clients pay for your guidance and support in achieving their goals.

- Public Speaking and Media Appearances:

As your personal brand gains recognition, you may receive invitations for media interviews, podcasts, or guest appearances on television or radio. These opportunities can enhance your visibility, establish credibility, and potentially lead to income-generating partnerships or collaborations.

It's important to build and nurture an engaged audience, consistently create valuable content, and maintain authenticity and trust with your followers. Remember to comply with legal and ethical guidelines, disclose sponsorships, and prioritize the needs and interests of your audience for long-term success in monetizing your personal brand on social media.

Chapter 5: Navigating Real Estate and Property Investment

Real Estate Investing

Real estate offers a range of investment options, each with its own characteristics, financing methods, and risk management considerations. Here are different real estate options, financing strategies, and risk management approaches to consider:

- Residential Real Estate:

Residential properties include single-family homes, townhouses, apartments, or condominiums. Financing options for residential real estate include:

a. Mortgage Loans: Obtain a mortgage loan from a bank or financial institution. This involves making a down payment and repaying the loan over a specific period, typically with interest.

b. Renting: Generate income by renting out residential properties to tenants. Rental income can cover mortgage payments and provide a passive income stream.

c. House Hacking: Purchase a multi-unit property and live in one unit while renting out the others. This allows you to generate rental income while living in the property, potentially covering mortgage expenses.

- Commercial Real Estate:

Commercial properties include office buildings, retail spaces, warehouses, or industrial properties. Financing options for commercial real estate include:

a. Commercial Mortgages: Similar to residential mortgages, commercial mortgages provide funding for purchasing or refinancing commercial properties. Lenders may require higher down payments and evaluate the property's income potential and market viability.

b. Commercial Leases: Generate income by leasing commercial properties to businesses. Leases can be long-term, providing stable cash flow.

- Real Estate Investment Trusts (REITs):

REITs are companies that own and manage income-generating real estate properties. Investing in REITs allows you to participate in real estate ownership without directly owning properties. REITs are traded on stock exchanges and provide dividends to investors.

- Real Estate Partnerships:

Participate in real estate partnerships, such as limited partnerships (LPs) or limited liability companies (LLCs). These structures allow multiple investors to pool their resources and invest in real estate projects collectively. Financing and risk management are shared among the partners.

- Real Estate Crowdfunding:

Invest in real estate through crowdfunding platforms. These platforms pool investments from multiple individuals to fund real estate projects. Investors can choose specific projects based on their investment goals and risk tolerance.

- Real Estate Development:

Participate in real estate development projects, such as constructing residential or commercial properties. Financing options for real estate development include construction loans or joint ventures with developers.

- Risk Management in Real Estate:

To manage risks associated with real estate investments, consider the following strategies:

a. Due Diligence: Conduct thorough research and analysis before investing in any real estate opportunity. Evaluate the property's location, market conditions, potential rental income, and potential risks.

b. Diversification: Diversify your real estate investments across different property types, locations, and investment strategies. This helps mitigate risk by spreading exposure to various market conditions.

c. Property Insurance: Protect your real estate investments with appropriate property insurance coverage. This helps mitigate risks associated with damage, liability, or other unforeseen events.

d. Cash Flow Analysis: Analyse potential rental income and expenses to ensure positive cash flow. Consider factors such as vacancies, maintenance costs, property management fees, and taxes.

e. Legal and Regulatory Compliance: Stay informed about local laws and regulations pertaining to real estate investments. Comply with zoning laws, building codes, rental regulations, and landlord-tenant laws to mitigate legal risks.

f. Professional Guidance: Seek advice from real estate professionals, including real estate agents, attorneys, and property managers. Their expertise can help you navigate complex transactions, contracts, and legal considerations.

It's important to conduct thorough research, assess your financial situation, and consult with professionals before investing in real estate. Consider your investment goals, risk tolerance, and the local real estate market conditions to make informed decisions.

Rental Properties

Becoming a successful landlord and creating consistent cash flow from rental properties requires careful planning, effective management, and a focus on tenant satisfaction. Here are some key strategies to help you achieve success in rental property ownership:

- Choose the Right Property:

Select a property with potential for rental income and appreciation. Consider factors such as location, market demand, proximity to amenities, and the condition of the property. Conduct thorough research and financial analysis to ensure the property aligns with your investment goals.

- Set Competitive Rental Rates:

Determine rental rates based on market conditions, comparable properties in the area, and the property's features and amenities. Avoid setting rents too high, as it may lead to extended vacancies. Conversely, setting rents too low could result in missed income opportunities.

- Screen Tenants:

Implement a rigorous tenant screening process to find reliable and responsible renters. Conduct background and credit checks, verify employment and income, and contact previous landlords for references. Selecting quality tenants reduces the risk of missed rent payments and property damage.

- Maintain the Property:

Regularly maintain and upkeep the property to attract and retain tenants. Promptly address maintenance issues, conduct regular inspections, and make necessary repairs. Well-maintained properties increase tenant satisfaction, reduce vacancies, and preserve property value.

- Develop Strong Tenant Relationships:

Establish good communication and rapport with tenants. Respond promptly to their concerns, address maintenance requests, and provide clear guidelines for property rules and expectations. Building positive tenant relationships encourages longer tenancies and minimizes turnover.

- Enforce Lease Agreements and Policies:

Ensure tenants understand and adhere to lease agreements and property policies. Clearly outline rules regarding rent payment deadlines, late fees, property maintenance responsibilities, and any restrictions or regulations. Consistently enforce these terms to maintain order and protect your interests.

- Market Vacancies Effectively:

Minimize vacancies by marketing your rental property effectively. Use online rental platforms, local classifieds, and social media to reach potential tenants. Highlight the property's features, location, and competitive rental terms. Consider professional photography and virtual tours to showcase the property.

- Regularly Review Rental Rates:

Stay updated on market rental rates and periodically review your rental rates. Adjust rents based on market conditions, inflation, property upgrades, or changes in the local rental market. Regularly evaluating and adjusting rental rates ensures you maximize your rental income.

- Seek Professional Property Management:

If managing the property becomes overwhelming or you lack the necessary time or expertise, consider hiring a professional property management company. They can handle tenant screening, rent collection, maintenance, and other day-to-day tasks, allowing you to focus on your other investments or interests.

- Account for Cash Flow and Expenses:

Maintain detailed financial records of your rental property income and expenses. Calculate your net operating income (NOI) by subtracting expenses (mortgage, property taxes, insurance, maintenance costs) from rental income. Ensure your rental income covers expenses and allows for a positive cash flow.

- Plan for Contingencies:

Set aside funds for unexpected expenses, such as major repairs, vacancies, or legal fees. Establish a reserve fund to handle these contingencies, ensuring you have the necessary resources to address unexpected financial burdens.

- Stay Compliant with Laws and Regulations:

Understand and comply with local landlord-tenant laws and regulations. Familiarize yourself with fair housing laws, eviction processes, property safety requirements, and other legal obligations. Staying compliant protects you from legal disputes and potential liabilities.

Remember, being a successful landlord requires ongoing commitment, proactive management, and a focus on tenant satisfaction. By providing quality properties, maintaining open communication, and managing your finances effectively, you can create consistent cash flow and build a profitable rental property portfolio.

Real Estate Investment Trusts (REITs)

Investing in Real Estate Investment Trusts (REITs) can be an effective way to gain exposure to the real estate market and potentially generate income. REITs are companies that own, operate, or finance income-generating real estate properties. Here are some key considerations when investing in REITs:

- Understand REIT Types:

There are different types of REITs, including equity REITs, mortgage REITs, and hybrid REITs. Equity REITs primarily own and operate income-producing properties, while mortgage REITs invest in real estate debt. Hybrid REITs combine elements of both equity and mortgage REITs. Each type has its own risk and return characteristics.

- Conduct Due Diligence:

Before investing in a specific REIT, conduct thorough research and due diligence. Evaluate the REIT's investment strategy, portfolio composition, management team, historical performance, and dividend payout history. Review their financial statements, annual reports, and other relevant disclosures.

- Evaluate Property Types and Locations:

Consider the property types and geographic locations in which the REIT invests. Different property sectors, such as residential, commercial, retail, or industrial, may perform differently based on market conditions and economic cycles. Assess the REIT's exposure to specific property sectors and determine if it aligns with your investment objectives.

- Assess Dividend Yield and Growth:

REITs are required by law to distribute a significant portion of their taxable income as dividends to shareholders. Evaluate the REIT's dividend yield, which indicates the annual dividend payout relative to the stock price. Additionally, assess the REIT's history of dividend growth to understand its ability to sustain and increase dividend payments over time.

- Consider Total Return Potential:

In addition to dividends, consider the potential for capital appreciation or total return. This involves assessing the REIT's growth prospects, property valuations, rental income potential, and market conditions. Total return combines dividend income and capital gains/ losses.

- Analyse Financial Metrics:

Analyse key financial metrics, such as funds from operations (FFO), net operating income (NOI), occupancy rates, and debt levels. FFO is a common measure of REIT profitability that adds depreciation and amortization to net income. Evaluate how these metrics have performed historically and compare them to industry benchmarks.

- Understand Risks:

Like any investment, REITs come with risks. Market conditions, interest rate changes, property valuations, tenant defaults, and regulatory changes can impact the performance of REITs. Assess the specific risks associated with the property sectors and locations in which the REIT operates.

- Diversify Your Portfolio:

Consider diversifying your real estate investments by investing in multiple REITs across different sectors and geographies. This helps reduce concentration risk and exposure to specific market conditions.

- Monitor Performance and Industry Trends:

Stay informed about the REIT's performance, industry trends, and economic indicators. Monitor financial news, reports, and updates from the REIT and broader real estate market. Regularly review the REIT's performance against your investment goals.

- Consult with a Financial Advisor:

If you are unsure about investing in REITs or need personalized advice, consult with a financial advisor or investment professional. They can help assess your risk tolerance, investment objectives, and provide guidance on REIT selection and portfolio construction.

Remember, investing in REITs carries market risk, and past performance is not indicative of future results. Carefully consider your investment goals, risk tolerance, and seek professional advice to make informed investment decisions.

Chapter 6: Building Wealth for the Long Term

Retirement Planning

Financial planning for retirement is crucial to ensure a comfortable and secure future. Here are key steps to consider when planning for retirement:

- Set Retirement Goals:

Define your retirement goals by considering factors such as the lifestyle you desire, desired retirement age, and anticipated expenses during retirement. This will help you determine the amount of money you need to save and the timeline for achieving your goals.

- Assess Your Current Financial Situation:

Evaluate your current financial situation, including your income, expenses, assets, debts, and investments. Determine your net worth and cash flow. This assessment will provide a baseline for creating your retirement plan.

- Estimate Retirement Expenses:

Estimate your future retirement expenses, taking into account both essential expenses (e.g., housing, healthcare, food) and discretionary expenses (e.g., travel, hobbies, entertainment). Consider inflation and potential healthcare costs when projecting your expenses.

- Calculate Retirement Income:

Determine your expected retirement income from various sources, such as pensions, Social Security, investment income, rental income, and annuities. Factor in any employer-sponsored retirement plans, such as a 401(k) or pension plan, and assess the impact of potential income streams.

- Bridge the Retirement Income Gap:

If there is a gap between your estimated retirement expenses and projected income, develop strategies to bridge that gap. This may involve increasing savings, extending your working years, or exploring additional income sources during retirement.

- Develop a Retirement Savings Plan:

Create a retirement savings plan by setting a target savings amount and establishing a timeline for reaching that goal. Consider tax-advantaged retirement accounts, such as Individual Retirement Accounts (IRAs) or employer-sponsored plans like 401(k)s. Determine how much you need to save regularly to achieve your desired retirement nest egg.

- Invest for Retirement:

Develop an investment strategy that aligns with your risk tolerance, time horizon, and retirement goals. Diversify your investments across different asset classes to manage risk. Regularly review and rebalance your portfolio to ensure it remains aligned with your objectives.

- Maximize Employer Benefits:

Take advantage of any employer-sponsored retirement benefits, such as matching contributions to retirement plans. Contribute at least enough to receive the maximum employer match, as it's essentially free money that boosts your retirement savings.

- Minimize Debt:

Strive to pay off high-interest debt, such as credit card balances or personal loans, before retirement. Minimizing debt reduces financial stress and allows you to allocate more resources towards savings and retirement income.

- Plan for Healthcare Costs:

Factor healthcare costs into your retirement plan. Consider health insurance options, including Medicare, and explore supplemental insurance policies to cover potential gaps. Contribute to a Health Savings Account (HSA) if eligible, as it offers tax advantages for future healthcare expenses.

- Review Insurance Coverage:

Review your insurance coverage, including life insurance and long-term care insurance. Evaluate whether adjustments are needed based on your retirement goals and risk tolerance.

- Monitor and Adjust:

Regularly monitor your retirement plan and make adjustments as needed. Review your progress, reassess your goals, and make necessary changes to your savings, investment strategy, or retirement timeline.

- Seek Professional Guidance:

Consider working with a certified financial planner (CFP) or retirement planning specialist who can provide personalized advice based on your unique circumstances. They can help optimize your retirement plan, navigate tax implications, and provide guidance on investment decisions.

Remember, retirement planning is an ongoing process. Regularly review and update your plan as your circumstances change and as you progress towards retirement. By starting early, saving consistently, and making informed financial decisions, you can work towards a financially secure and fulfilling retirement.

Wealth Preservation

Protecting wealth and ensuring a lasting legacy involves thoughtful planning and strategic measures to preserve and transfer assets to future generations. Here are key considerations to protect your wealth and establish a lasting legacy:

- Estate Planning:

Develop a comprehensive estate plan that includes a will, trust(s), power of attorney, and healthcare directives. Consult with an estate planning attorney to ensure your assets are distributed according to your wishes and in a tax-efficient manner. Regularly review and update your estate plan to reflect any changes in your family, financial situation, or laws.

- Asset Protection Strategies:

Implement asset protection strategies to safeguard your wealth from potential risks, creditors, or legal claims. These may include the use of trusts, limited liability companies (LLCs), or other legal entities. Asset protection measures can help shield your wealth from personal or business liabilities.

- Insurance Coverage:

Maintain appropriate insurance coverage to protect your assets and mitigate risks. This may include homeowners' insurance, umbrella liability insurance, life insurance, and long-term care insurance. Regularly review your insurance policies to ensure they adequately cover your assets and liabilities.

- Business Succession Planning:

If you own a business, develop a succession plan to ensure a smooth transition of ownership and management to the next generation or a chosen successor. Consider tax implications, training and development of successors, and the ongoing viability and growth of the business.

- Charitable Giving:

Incorporate philanthropy into your wealth management and legacy planning. Establish a charitable giving plan that aligns with your values and philanthropic goals. Options include setting up a foundation, donor-advised funds, or including charitable bequests in your estate plan.

- Education and Financial Literacy:

Empower future generations by promoting education and financial literacy within your family. Teach children and grandchildren about responsible money management, investing, and the value of philanthropy. Encourage lifelong learning and provide resources to foster financial independence and success.

- Family Governance:

Consider establishing a family governance structure to facilitate effective communication, decision-making, and wealth transfer among family members. This may involve family meetings, the creation of a family mission statement, or the appointment of a family council to manage family assets and foster unity.

- Continuity Planning:

Develop a continuity plan to ensure the smooth management of your affairs in the event of incapacity or unexpected circumstances. This may include designating trusted individuals as power of attorney, setting up living trusts, and documenting your wishes for medical care and end-of-life decisions.

- Regular Review and Professional Advice:

Regularly review and update your wealth protection and legacy planning strategies as your circumstances change. Seek advice from professionals such as attorneys, accountants, and financial advisors who specialize in wealth management and estate planning. They can provide guidance and help you navigate complex legal and financial matters.

- Open Communication:

Maintain open and honest communication with your family members about your wealth, values, and intentions. Discuss your legacy goals, estate plans, and any expectations or responsibilities. Clear communication can help minimize potential conflicts and ensure a smooth transition of wealth and values to future generations.

Remember, protecting wealth and establishing a lasting legacy requires a holistic approach that considers legal, financial, and personal aspects. By implementing proactive strategies, seeking professional advice, and nurturing family relationships, you can preserve your wealth and leave a meaningful legacy for generations to come.

Impact Investing

Socially responsible investing (SRI), also known as sustainable investing or ethical investing, involves aligning investment decisions with personal values and social or environmental considerations. SRI aims to generate financial returns while also making a positive impact on society and the environment. Here are key aspects of socially responsible investing:

- Environmental, Social, and Governance (ESG) Factors:

ESG factors are used to evaluate the sustainability and ethical impact of an investment. Environmental factors assess a company's impact on the environment, such as carbon emissions or resource usage. Social factors consider labour practices, human rights, diversity, and community impact. Governance factors evaluate the quality of a company's leadership, transparency, and shareholder rights.

- Screening and Selection:

SRI involves applying specific criteria to screen potential investments. Negative screening excludes companies involved in industries such as tobacco, weapons, or fossil fuels. Positive screening focuses on selecting companies that demonstrate positive environmental, social, or governance practices. Some investors also utilize thematic investing, targeting specific issues like clean energy or gender equality.

- Shareholder Advocacy:

Engagement with companies through shareholder advocacy involves using shareholder rights to influence corporate behaviour. This can include dialogues with management, proxy voting on ESG-related resolutions, and submitting proposals to improve company practices. Shareholder advocacy aims to encourage companies to adopt more sustainable and responsible practices.

- Impact Investing:

Impact investing goes beyond SRI by intentionally seeking investments that generate positive social or environmental impact alongside financial returns. It involves directing capital towards projects or companies with specific social or environmental goals, such as renewable energy projects, affordable housing initiatives, or microfinance programs.

- Community Investing:

Community investing focuses on supporting underserved communities or marginalized groups by providing capital to organizations that address social or economic needs. This can involve investing in community development banks, credit unions, or community development financial institutions (CDFIs) that provide financing to businesses and projects in disadvantaged areas.

- ESG Integration:

ESG integration involves incorporating environmental, social, and governance factors into traditional investment analysis. By evaluating these factors alongside financial metrics, investors can better assess the long-term sustainability and risk profile of an investment. ESG integration aims to capture the potential financial benefits of considering non-financial factors.

- Performance and Returns:

SRI has demonstrated that responsible investments can deliver competitive financial returns. Research suggests that companies with strong ESG practices may outperform their peers over the long term. However, it's important to note that financial returns can vary depending on the specific investment strategy, market conditions, and individual investment choices.

- Reporting and Transparency:

SRI advocates for increased transparency and disclosure from companies regarding their ESG practices. Investors seek comprehensive and standardized reporting on ESG factors to make informed investment decisions. Efforts are underway to establish globally recognized reporting frameworks, such as the Global Reporting Initiative (GRI) and the Sustainability Accounting Standards Board (SASB).

- Professional Guidance:

Considering the complexity of SRI, consulting with a financial advisor or investment professional specializing in sustainable investing can be beneficial. They can help align your investment goals with your values, provide insights on responsible investment options, and assess the ESG practices of investment opportunities.

Remember that socially responsible investing is a broad and evolving field, and individual preferences for what constitutes responsible investing can vary. Conduct thorough research, review available investment options, and consult with professionals to align your investment approach with your values and financial goals.

Giving Back

Philanthropy plays a crucial role in society and has a significant impact on addressing societal challenges, promoting social well-being, and creating positive change. Here are some key reasons why philanthropy is important:

- Addressing Social Issues:

Philanthropy enables individuals and organizations to support causes they are passionate about and make a difference in areas such as education, healthcare, poverty alleviation, environmental conservation, and more. It fills gaps where public resources may be limited and allows for targeted interventions to tackle pressing social issues.

- Making a Positive Impact:

Philanthropy provides an opportunity to create a positive impact on communities and individuals. By investing time, resources, and expertise, philanthropists can support initiatives that improve lives, empower marginalized groups, promote social justice, and contribute to sustainable development.

- Driving Innovation and Research:

Philanthropic support often fuels innovation, research, and development in various fields. By funding scientific research, technological advancements, and creative endeavours, philanthropy helps drive progress, expand knowledge, and find solutions to complex challenges.

- Catalysing Change and Advocacy:

Philanthropy can play a vital role in catalysing systemic change and advocating for social justice. By supporting organizations and initiatives focused on policy reform, advocacy campaigns, and community mobilization, philanthropists can contribute to positive societal transformations and promote a more equitable and inclusive society.

- Filling Funding Gaps:

Philanthropy can fill funding gaps that public institutions or traditional funding sources may not adequately address. Nonprofit organizations, social enterprises, and community-based initiatives often rely on philanthropic support to deliver critical services, implement programs, and sustain their operations.

- Leveraging Resources and Networks:

Philanthropists can leverage their resources, expertise, and networks to drive collective action and foster collaborations. By bringing together stakeholders from various sectors—nonprofits, businesses, government entities, and community leaders—philanthropy can facilitate partnerships and amplify the impact of philanthropic efforts.

- Inspiring Others and Cultivating a Culture of Giving:

Philanthropy has the power to inspire and influence others to give back. When individuals or organizations lead by example and showcase the impact of their philanthropic endeavours, it encourages others to contribute their time, skills, and resources. Philanthropy helps cultivate a culture of giving and fosters a sense of collective responsibility for the well-being of society.

- Personal Fulfilment and Legacy:

Engaging in philanthropy can provide a sense of personal fulfilment and purpose. It allows individuals to align their values with their actions, leave a meaningful legacy, and create a positive imprint on the world. Philanthropy offers an opportunity to contribute to something greater than oneself and leave a lasting impact for future generations.

It's important to approach philanthropy with thoughtful planning, due diligence, and a focus on long-term impact. Engage in strategic giving, research organizations or causes you wish to support, and consider collaborating with trusted partners or experts in the field to maximize the effectiveness of your philanthropic efforts.

Milton Keynes UK
Ingram Content Group UK Ltd.
UKHW022204221223
434840UK00015B/648